THE FIRST FIFTY

THE
First Fifty
Munro-Bagging Without A Beard
Muriel Gray

MAINSTREAM
PUBLISHING
EDINBURGH AND LONDON

First published in Great Britain in 1991 by
MAINSTREAM PUBLISHING COMPANY (EDINBURGH) LTD
7 Albany Street
Edinburgh EH1 3UG

British Library Cataloguing in Publication Data
Gray, Muriel
    The First Fifty: Munro-Bagging without a Beard
    1. Scotland. Highlands. Mountains. Munros. Hill-walking
    I. Title
    796.522

ISBN 1-85158-353-X
ISBN 1-85158-389-0 pbk

Photographs © Ross Murray: pages 8–9, 43, 172–3, 175, 176–7 and 188–9
Photographs © Rod Stein: pages 16, 23, 41, 144–5, 148, 180, 181, 184 and 185
Photographs © Dennis Hardley: pages 36, 68–9, 128–9, 133 and 160–1
Additional photography by Muriel Gray

Design by James Hutcheson, Edinburgh
Origination by Marshall Thomson Colour Reproduction Ltd, Edinburgh
Typeset in 11/13pt Garamond by Falcon Typographic Art Ltd, Edinburgh and London
Printed in Great Britain by Butler and Tanner Ltd, Frome, Somerset

Contents

To those I love, who shared
their soup with me at the cairn

Introduction

IF YOU WALK UP MOUNTAINS FOR FUN, THEN A GOOD IDEA IS TO KEEP the dark secret to yourself when it comes to birthdays or Christmas. The reason is that relations and friends put you into the 'easy' category of present buying, which is probably why you're miserably flicking through this book.

They will automatically take their cheque book into an outdoor shop. This is not a shop that trades beneath a flapping canvas on the edge of the pavement, but a shop where even the carpet is made of Gortex, and the assistants shift restlessly from one trainer-clad foot to another as they dream of being somewhere other than here beneath the striplit rows of anoraks and attractive wall displays of bum-bags.

These shops also display books on climbing and walking, and perhaps you're reading this bit as you stand in such a shop somewhere between the ice-axes and the fuchsia skiing tube socks. The problem is that your friends and relations will quickly lose patience in trying to decide if you already have a Swiss army knife, or whether a hat with a pompom may get you beaten up in the Kingshouse Hotel, and just go for the easy option of buying you a book with a man with a beard on the cover. You can't go wrong with books that have men with beards on them. I know. Relations have bought me hundreds. The man will be on top of a particularly dramatic-looking mountain, and no matter how pompously the hairy author writes about his tedious exploits and mind-numbingly dull companions, the book will always be bought for the pictures. So just as you may have flicked through old *National Geographic* magazines as a teenager looking for the pictures of naked tribes with huge breasts and penises, you can flick through the bearded man's book looking for interesting peaks and scary photographs of people hanging off rocks.

To satisfy your lust for drama just such a photo is shown overleaf.

I shan't be at all offended if you now flick through to see what hills I've decided to discuss and decide you most certainly never want to read or own such a book. After all, it's not important if you like or dislike it. Your Aunty Helen or your flat-mate Alan will almost certainly buy it for you next time you have a birthday and you will have to thank them and put it in the warehouse with the rest of the outdoor books.

Tough titty. You should have taken up golf.

Why Me?

YOU REMEMBER YOUR FIRST MOUNTAIN IN MUCH THE SAME WAY YOU remember having your first sexual experience, except that walking doesn't make as much mess and you don't cry for a week if Ben Nevis forgets to phone next morning.

But, like losing your virginity, it's hard to recreate that nascent flavour of exhilaration when you realise that by determination, corporeal suffering that involves wheezing until your lungs feel like a laboratory beagle's, you've done something you didn't believe physically possible. Unfortunately, unlike losing your virginity, Munro-bagging stays just as sore every time you do it.

To the sofa-bound layperson it may just be a wind-blown cairn, grey and dismal except for its decorative orange peel, but to you it's nirvana. It remains constantly awe-inspiring that your feet, and a flask of tomato soup, can take you to the remotest and most primevally beautiful parts of our country, from where those who sit in aluminium chairs a foot from an open hatchback listening to Gary Davis's *Bit In the Middle* are excluded by their sedentary nature. It's a sensation that once felt has to be repeated for the rest of your life, or until the end of Gary Davis's *Bit In the Middle*, whichever comes first.

Ben Arthur, or The Cobbler, was my first. Not a Munro, but 15 years ago, at the tender age of 16 when I should have been in Sauchiehall Street choosing stripey socks, I could be forgiven for never having heard of Sir Hugh or his damned tables. Never mind Munros – had I known how hard The Cobbler was to be I would have stayed home and watched a black-and-white movie on telly with my mum. To this day I am the kind of hill-walker who starts the day with a face like a football with slits cut in it for eyes. The early start so essential to claiming that peak has never become easier. But to impress the man I loved at the time, I emerged from his friend's beat-up Mini at the car park opposite Arrochar thinking, 'I am not going to lose this very handsome boyfriend who wants to do this instead of going to Kelvingrove Art Gallery for a look at the Rembrandt and a snog. I will die as soon as we start to walk.

'He's bound to leave me to rot,' I surmised, 'and get off with that tart from the textiles department at Glasgow School of Art that seemed to fancy him. I'll bet she goes hill-walking,' I thought as I caught sight of my figure in a donkey jacket and waterproof trousers in the car's wing mirror. Mind you, with thighs like a Tyrannosaurus Rex I suppose the brazen hussy would have been well suited to the hills, and I bet even her hair would mat like felt under a balaclava for eight hours.

So I admit it was sex that drove me on that winter's day, through rain at first, turning to sleet as we passed the tree line and into wet driving snow as we neared the top.

Winter hill-climbing has tortures all of its own. Never go first in thick snow unless you have legs that are six feet long and thighs of iron. Breaking the path is murder. For some reason I imagined this was my task, kicking pathetic little holes up the gradient with all the effectiveness of a toddler having a tantrum in a supermarket.

In those days of misplaced student feminism I was terrified of being seen as a feeble girlie. God knows why. These days I'd sing *On the Good Ship Lollipop* and speak like Bonnie Langford if I could get one of the lazy bastards with beards to carry my rucksack. Unfortunately, 20th-century men are shrewd, reserving their manly acts of chivalry only for those who resemble Brooke Shields. Since my hair does indeed mat like felt under a balaclava, I usually end up carrying their rucksacks.

But, way back then, I genuinely believed that physical weakness was a sign of inferiority, and so I would struggle away, silently hyperventilating to keep up with these men who weighed 13 stone next to my eight stone, and whose legs were so big they could get to the top in three strides.

Wrestling with the thought 'I want to go back' is fundamental to hill-walking, and of course all the bearded experts with accents like Sussex vicars will advise you that you must always know when to turn back. If you are 16 and trying to get your boyfriend to think you're great, the answer is that you may only turn back when all the other members of the party before you have lost two or more of their limbs and decide it's time to call it a day.

I imagined it with horror.

'I see you've lost a leg there, Ian.'

'Aye, Alec, but it's OK. It's only knocked the schedule out by ten minutes. We'll be at the top in an hour. How's that grievous spinal injury you've just incurred?'

'No problem, Ian. I'll just crawl up to this coll with my one good arm and take a bearing. Is that Ladhar Bheinn over there or are the severe facial lacerations I have been unlucky enough to receive clouding my vision? Any Lucozade left?'

This too has changed in my maturity. Now I make sure we travel in my car. There is no greater incentive for calling the shots than cheerily telling the chaps who want to continue up a mountain in a force-ten gale and blizzard that they may make their own way back from Torridon to Glasgow.

However, I digress. Struggling up The Cobbler as I was on that day, I was not only wrestling with the thought 'I want to go back', I had started to form the thought 'Perhaps I'll die'. The worst aspect of this thought at 16 is that Mountain Rescue may remove your balaclava before you've got to a hair brush. 'Nasty,' the mountain leader would say. 'Hair matted like felt.'

But no one had explained the pain barrier to me at that age. It is the most astonishing feeling, that only someone as chronically unfit as I am can experience, to come through the painful fog into the bright sunlight of new energy. The medical explanation is to do with metabolism and stamina. My explanation is that I remembered there were to be pork pies soon. The arrival at the top of that small hill meant everything to me. Not only lunch and a chance to sit down on a rock, but the fact that in spite of my grossly sedentary nature, I was actually there on the snowy summit with the boys.

What could have been more thrilling and rewarding than to have conquered pain, exhaustion and the humiliation of looking like a navigational engineer, to stand on this beautiful, silent top drinking in the view across Loch Long to Ben Lomond? I was elated, and have continued to be every time I haul myself to the summit of anything higher than the top deck of a bus.

It seems ludicrous now that I found such a short walk so arduous. But it's important to realise that most teenage girls take exercise only when dancing round their handbags at discos looking for men over six feet. Stamina is often psychological and if you wander the Munros in

13

all seasons, you'll find yourself calling on it in a bewildering variety of situations.

I'm grateful that it was a boyfriend who gave me that first taste of the hills, and not my parents. I often come across small family units wandering through the heather, a tweedy university lecturer of a father setting the pace, followed at a respectful distance by a bespectacled, lank-haired mother wearing an acrylic hat and towing two sulky miserable children. Judging by their disgruntled demeanour, these poor mites will doubtless stop walking the hills the moment they grow their first pubic hair, and I grieve for all the pleasure they will miss as adults if they put the hills aside as one would childhood caravan holidays in Girvan. Only take your children up mountains if they beg and scream to go. A pleasure you discover for yourself is worth far more than one you were expected to enjoy by your elders. And how can you enjoy a cold pint in the bar afterwards if you're only seven and a half?

Apart from anything else, hill-walking is not quite as wholesome as our bearded, Fair Isle tank-top brigade would have us believe, so exposing your children to some of the tartan-shirted bears one finds relieving themselves behind cairns is perhaps to be avoided.

So The Cobbler got me going and I haven't stopped since.

I am always mortally offended when people express surprise that I am a keen mountaineer. I have no idea why a job in television should give strangers the impression that my idea of fun is to hang around night clubs sniffing nose candy. But they most definitely register disappointment when I tell them that I'd swop without hesitation a ticket to some God-awful film première and party that minor celebrities are expected to attend, for a night by the log fire at the Cluanie Inn discussing whether the South Kintail Ridge really deserves to have seven Munros.

I have great pity and sympathy for my misguided colleagues who imagine they are living the high life in London, mooching from champagne reception to book launch party in the grim pursuit of having their photograph in a Sunday supplement magazine alongside a member of the England football squad. That is as near to my idea of Hell as possible, perhaps with the exception of being stuck in a lift with Simon Bates.

I can think of no greater privilege than to be able to live and work in Scotland, where at every possible opportunity one is able to jump into a car and head for one of the most beautiful and accessible areas of wilderness in the world. In the same time it takes someone to get from Central London to Heathrow airport in a Hackney cab with a fascist behind the wheel, I can be cruising over Drumochter Summit well on my way to Heaven. I can only thank my parents from the bottom of my soul for not bringing me up in Belgium.

So this is not a guide book, but a grateful celebration of something I love. Indeed sometimes when I find myself all alone amidst scenery so grand and profoundly inspiring that it sweetly forces me to examine my life and values, love is almost an inadequate word. Experience is really only a series of near misses and major triumphs from which you learn, and the only way to become a competent mountaineer is to scramble up mountains in every possible weather, and in every season.

Hopefully those of you who want to start wandering in the wilderness, but who for one reason or another are unable or unwilling to grow a beard, will be encouraged by the fact that someone as unlikely as the spindly-legged little sprat that I am, has done so. I offer you my observations only as an amateur, and will be delighted if they encourage you to explore and fall in love with the mountains of Scotland. That is, unless you're a complete dick-head that leaves litter at the top, parks on farmers' private roads and doesn't care what mountain you're on as long as you can tick it off in the book. Please put this book down immediately, it isn't meant for you. You'll be after the train-spotting volumes which you'll find over there next to the pet care books.

The rest of you may read on.

The mountain that started it all: The Cobbler

You Mean You Do It For Fun?

ALTHOUGH YOU'RE PROBABLY SICK OF HAVING DULL OLD BUFFERS IN moleskin breeches telling you how the hills are full of very different people than they remember, it happens to be true. When the Scottish Mountaineering Club brought out a comprehensive guide cunningly titled *The Munros* in 1985, little did they suspect that the XR2 drivers would steer their crates away from the ski-slopes and head for the un-pisted hills – hills previously only visited by those of us who smugly regarded them as a spiritual escape, a haven of solitude, rather than a sport requiring the purchase of expensive consumer durables and matching accessories.

I had no idea what a Munro was when I started mountaineering. Hence years later a mad-eyed fellow walker in a bar at Crianlarich surprised me by expressing dismay on my behalf that I had 'wasted all that time' climbing up lesser peaks like the mountains of Assynt, and been foolish in the extreme to have scaled some peaks several times as I had, and indeed still do. The real challenge, I was told by this loony, was to complete the Munros. I thought he meant a chain of butcher shops and my mind raced as to why I would be required to visit meat shops around the country examining best cuts of Scottish lamb. I was put in the picture. The chap wasn't quite sure who Munro was, but he was sure about one thing. Other peaks don't count, he informed me conspiratorially, wiping the foam of his Guinness from his beard.

And so, as if by prophecy, the SMC's book appeared in every walker's Christmas stocking, mocking my expeditions up smaller but beloved mountains. Here at last was a book listing all the Munros, giving the reader the perfect tool of one-upmanship. 'How many have you done?' echoed in the beer bars of major cities.

Just as lots of men waste thousands of hours and pounds pointlessly on hi-fi equipment, since all they do is get home and play Dire Straits, so did lots of men spend thousands of pounds and hours on Gortex creations, boots, tents, axes and foil bags, only to trudge about on boring lumps in the mist to get another unpronounceable name ticked off in the SMC's book.

No, of course they wouldn't dream of going up Suilven. It's not a Munro, is it? Much better to tick off something a couple of hundred feet higher even if it's as exciting as walking about on the roof of the Scottish Exhibition Centre.

Suddenly there was no talk of the beauty of the hill, wildlife encounters, or comparisons with other peaks in the bars at the foot of favourite mountains. Instead the properties of Yeti-gaiters were discussed religiously, cars were sized up and anecdotes about each other's very interesting jobs in computers were swopped. And above all, there was the burning question. 'How many have you done?'

But who can blame Mrs Thatcher's young consumers for wanting a bit of wilderness too? After all, I've been tutted at often enough on the hill by the beards, presumably for being a bottle blonde with a bit of lip salve on. And sometimes it can be a relief to meet these consumer magazine fanatics at the top if all you've met so far is a miserable family who look like depressed social workers. It's almost comforting listening to Maitland and Crawford talking about £1,500 solar rucksacks, after half an hour at a cairn listening to Mr Social Worker make the two junior social workers name alpine flowers they've spotted on the way up in alphabetical order.

'It was a Cryptogramma crispa, Daddy!'

'That's correct, Rebecca, now write it down in your notebook and eat your lentils.'

Economics have certainly changed the face of the modern mountaineer. No longer exclusively an escape from the dole queue in Glasgow, it's now an escape from the office, and a sport to discuss over the dinner tables of Hyndland along with windsurfing and skiing.

But if the original pioneering mountain men have seen radical changes since they strode in a manly fashion up the crags in the 30s, the changes since the 70s have been just as fascinating, in more than just economic terms.

The mountains really were the domain of men. Men who roamed in noisy packs wearing tartan shirts, who prided themselves on their hardiness, and who sniggered about the women left at home in the same way Les Dawson discusses his mother-in-law.

But over the last two decades couples started sneaking on to the hill. Women decided that the men coming home flushed and excited and smelling of 80 shilling had been spending a more exciting day than the one they'd been wasting window-shopping for pine dressers. Articles about the great outdoors started to appear in women's magazines between the shortbread recipes and the advice on orgasms. Hence the hairy tartan pack members started to find that their wives and girlfriends wanted to come too, and the matching his and hers kagoul came into its own.

Of course the older Arran-knit-jumper couples, who contribute to the letters page in the *Scots Magazine* with photographs of peculiarly shaped rocks they've observed, had always been there. I have great affection for them. They've been sharing binoculars for years in the pursuit of the snow-bunting and a good spot to brew up.

The couples new to the ridges were quite different. Students, young marrieds, young professional couples who should have been watching the rugby or out buying compact discs. They had cars and could afford to stay in hotels, preferring to put on some casual cottons from Next in the evening and take their meals in the dining-room, instead of standing in the bar eating cheese toasties beside gently reeking climbers.

I started to notice them when I became aware of people staring at my donkey jacket in the car park. I also noticed that the women never wore balaclavas. The great pity is that this is practically the only time one sees women on the hills. The male tartan packs are still there, presumably having persuaded their women that a pine dresser is an important purchase, but there is no equivalent pack of women roaming the heather smelling of talcum powder instead of sweat and curry.

I'm as guilty. I only ever go to the hills with a man, a group of mixed sex friends or completely alone. I can't recall ever walking with a large group of women.

I don't think there is a sinister reason for this, merely a traditional social one. Walking expeditions are usually arranged in the pub, when someone, invariably a man, will express a desire to conquer a particular ridge or peak. This is followed by a debate on how to get there and a telephone poll of those one knows to be interested and free to go. Women, for whatever reason, are only ever included in this rounding up if they are one half of a climbing or walking couple. Often, like my first hill-walk, the women would be there under sufferance and struggling away on their own trying hard not to let the side down. I know this is changing, not just because my

female friends have all now bought their pine dressers, but because fleecy tops now come in pink.

I know women now who leave the men standing with their speed up a hill, and who can be relied on to take map bearings far more accurately in the mist than their hairier companions. But I'm anxious that more women realise that just because the whole mountaineering scene reeks with testosterone, an atmosphere that is irritatingly and continually promoted by all the most celebrated climbers and walkers, they should not exclude themselves from the joys of the hills. It's hopeless saying to women who don't get invited on walks by male friends, join a club. I would rather have my nipples cut off than have to sit in a mini-bus with a bunch of people who ask the driver to turn off the radio and think committees are a good idea, in the vain attempt to find kindred spirits. Fine if you want to stop for a nice cup of tea on the way home and discuss toilet facilities in Gairloch, but perhaps not the place to find wild, exciting and funny companions who can be reckless and responsible at the same time. I will of course stand corrected if someone can prove they met Harrison Ford on a mass ramble up Lochnagar, but my experience of organised walking clubs has been less than satisfactory for someone who wants to push themselves to the edge of their ability, and have a hoot in the pub later.

The best advice I can offer is to start walking with someone more experienced, man or woman, and then after about 20 mountains break loose and go on your own. Nothing will give you more confidence as a mountaineer than to have successfully taken decisions on your own, and to have experienced the true nature of solitude by having no one to half a Mars Bar with. For inexperienced and insecure women, this is the best way to gain confidence to initiate hill-walks instead of just waiting to see where the lads are off to this weekend and tagging along. Hopefully, if enough women wake up to the fact the hills are for them, then we'll see another swing away from the traditional macho mountaineer image that Munro-bagging has yet to escape from.

I certainly don't want men to start spending their Saturdays shopping for pine furniture instead of us. I just ache for a better balance of social and sexual mix on the hills; young women as well as young men, and people without money alongside those who can't get out of their Volvo unless their Gortex jacket matches their gaiters.

Having said that, don't all choose the same Munro at once, especially if it's one of my favourites. I'm getting cheesed off pursuing solitude, only to find the summit of a mountain less like a wind-blown sanctuary of peace, and more like the check-in desk for Palma at Glasgow airport on Fair Friday.

But then, in eulogising about my love of the mountains and my desire for the democratisation of their walkers, I forgot to mention one tiny thing. I'm a grumpy, selfish old cow and I want the hills to myself.

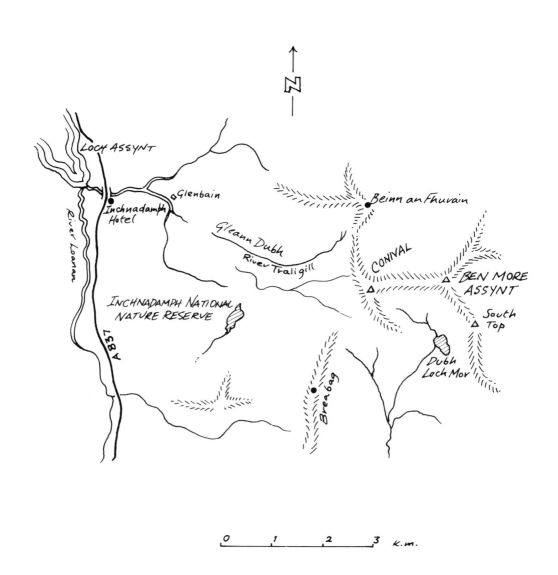

N

LOCH ASSYNT

Glenbain

Beinn an Fhurain

River Loanan

Inchnadamph
Hotel

Gleann Dubh

River Traligill

CONIVAL

BEN MORE
ASSYNT

INCHNADAMPH NATIONAL
NATURE RESERVE

South
Top

A837

Dubh
Loch Mor

Breabag

0   1   2   3   k.m.

Ben More Assynt to Conival

Ben More Assynt; 998m; (OS Sheet 15; 318201); M140.
Conival; 987m; (OS Sheet 15; 303199); M154.

I LOVE WALKING ALONE, BUT SOMETIMES MISS HAVING SOMEONE TO SHARE
it all with. For a start, how can you enjoy the standard argument at
the summit about the identity of the peaks you can see? Few mountain
tiffs are more heated than two or more hill-walkers fighting to make the
others realise why that can't possibly be Ben Nevis over there, or to be the
first one to correctly name the pointy little sod all on its own on the far
horizon. In such a squabble the answer is always Schiehallion. Remember
that. It saves time.

I decided to spend a few days off work one September, walking on my
own. I fancied Assynt, but then I have always fancied Assynt. If Assynt
was a boy I'd have knocked it to the ground with a rugby tackle and pulled
its trousers down years ago.

The most magnificent aspect of this wild area is its savage moorland, flat
but pitted with sparkling water-lily-clogged lochans, interrupted by curious
peaks that assume a grandeur far in excess of their true height. Plus it bears
a sublime coastline, white sand and a tumbling turquoise ocean that would
make poets weep. Certainly Norman MacCaig wrote about it extensively,
Assynt being an area that has touched him through decades. I'm not sure
if he weeps about the coastline, but I'll bet he's had a paddle.

The fascination of the area is endless, from the delights of a magnificent
coast road from Lochinver to Kylesku via Drumbeg, to the impressive Eas
a' Chual Aluinn waterfall at the head of Loch Glencoul, and of course the
breathtakingly extravagant mountain architecture.

One rather melancholy aspect is that its perfection has attracted the
variety of tourists who do not wish to go home and who have gradually

but steadily replaced the locals over the last 20 years. It's impossible for someone locally born and bred, invariably with a low-paid job, to compete on the property market with those who can realise over £100,000 for a shabby little terraced house in London. Hence few owners of houses, shops, hotels or petrol stations boast anything remotely like a Scottish accent. But if you can live with the reality that Sutherland is now a region in Surrey, then the incongruity of the new inhabitants will not mar your pleasure in beholding the majestic terrain amidst which they arrange their lawns round stone herons and name their ex-croft houses 'Windsor'. Who can blame them? Had I lived all my life in a rurally uninspiring, overpopulated country like England, I daresay I would be whimpering to live in Sutherland. I just can't help wondering as more and more elderly non-Scots buy holiday and retirement homes there, where the elderly locals are retiring to.

Since I'd scrambled up all the sexiest visible peaks like Quinag, Stac Pollaidh, Canisp and Suilven, and since Munro fever was newly burning in my veins, I headed for the two sneaky Munros hiding behind the Inchnadamph National Nature Reserve: Ben More Assynt and Conival.

The obvious starting point for the walk is from the Inchnadamph Hotel, and if you have enough cash to stay there it couldn't be more convenient. It's not wildly expensive but it's by no means a climbers' pit either. I arrived to find lots of elderly couples in suits and twin-sets taking sherry alongside dour fishermen. I had hoped for a bar full of burly, handsome geology students, since Assynt is a geological Mecca for those handy with a little hammer. But university term hadn't started so I was stranded in an atmosphere not dissimilar to an *Antiques Road Show* in Swindon.

I'm not sure if I dribble maniacally while I eat, but I have begun to notice that whenever I travel alone people completely ignore me. Hence when I finished my breakfast the following day and pulled on my boots, I had spoken only twice in 24 hours: once to apologise to a policeman for dreamily doing 68 mph on a single carriageway on the A9, for which I was forgiven, and secondly to check in and ask when dinner was.

Everybody else spoke to everybody else at dinner. In fact they were practically exchanging addresses across tables by the time the coffee was served. Even the waitress ignored me, choosing to ask the old couple at a table some distance away if they had enjoyed their lunch in Lochinver, while absently taking my order. It's worth remembering something before you set out for the Highlands with a romantic notion of bustling, lively inns, crackling log fires, impromptu music and song, and wise local characters to inform and amuse you about their landscape. Almost all Scottish hotels are like municipal old folk's homes, with miserable-looking senior citizens propped up in chilly residents' lounges waiting for an afternoon tea or a run to the nearest town in their beige Maestro. Soup of the day is always tomato and the fireplaces will be bricked up and sporting a one-bar coal-effect electric monstrosity that you will need permission to switch on. Of course I do not accuse the Inchnadamph Hotel of following such form, and I'm sure when it's full of students pouring beer over their heads and trying to abseil down to breakfast from the second floor, it can be a warm, lively little place. However, on the occasion of my visit I would have had more fun staying in a survival bag in the car park.

I took the packed lunch and silently set off up the farm track at the back of the hotel, leaving the other residents to plan which lay-by they would choose, where they could open the car doors a little and read a newspaper until it would be time to return for afternoon tea and scones.

You can see a grand Victorian house on your left on the other side of the river as you walk, but it's not the most important one in the area. The Vestey family, who own all the juiciest parts of Assynt, have a lodge at the back of Lochinver on the way to Suilven. Called Glencanisp Lodge, it's set in beautiful grounds with a loch that reflects the mountain perfectly into their sitting-room on the odd occasion when there's anyone there to enjoy it. So if you want to scowl at the herbacious borders of fabulously rich absentee landlords, it's an ideal spot to mooch past and sulk.

The walk into Conival is very straightforward, but I was irritated that I failed to find the caves marked on the ordnance survey map on the southern side of Gleann Dubh, and I dared not retrace my steps for fear of leaving insufficient time to complete both peaks. This is a hot area for potholing, a pastime only marginally more baffling than why people think Jim Davidson is funny. I put this to some potholers once.

'Well why do you go up hills?' they riposted smugly.

'Because it mixes the challenge of strenuous exercise with the reward of an amazing view, a fuller understanding of the geography of our land and intoxicating amounts of fresh air.'

'Oh,' they said, and became disappointingly silent, leaving me to this day waiting for a plausible excuse for their cramming themselves into hideous, airless, dangerously confined spaces with no certainty that there's a way out. Mind you, people do that on a daily basis when they travel British

Rail. At least the potholers get to wear a helmet with a light on it and don't have to listen to a bored Yorkshireman read out the entire buffet menu each time a luckless passenger joins the train.

So I missed the caves but plodded on up the narrowing track, making the peculiar mistake of crossing the river and climbing straight up a huge boulder field. I noticed two people were behind me at some distance, but just in case they had binoculars I stopped and tapped one of the rocks professionally, as if I meant to be there. Don't take my route whatever you do. The SMC book quite correctly tells you to follow the glen up on to the ridge, and if you shun that advice and copy my route you too would be floundering around on a near-vertical field of unstable and slippery rocks designed specially by God to break legs.

The slight detour only made the top sweeter, and after the confines of the glen, Conival surprises by its marvellously open aspect. From here you can see across to the Glencanisp forest and, more rewardingly, into the wild interior lands to the east. These really are hidden peaks since they cannot be viewed from the road and, indeed, Ben More will not come into view until you have claimed Conival. But if not as dramatic as some of their lower fellow mountains in the area, they are comely grey, scree-topped peaks, and stunning in the vantage point they offer to view vast tracts of Sutherland's wilderness unseen by the tourist.

The logical route to Ben More Assynt means carrying on round the ridge and then retracing your steps back to Conival for the descent. For variety and a much bigger walk, a fit Munroist could descend on the east side of Ben More, skirting the edge of Beinn an Fhurain to pick up a stalkers' path at Loch nan Cuaran.

However, I was rather looking forward to meeting the couple I could see gaining on me as I left Conival for Ben More. I worked out that if I had my lunch on the summit of Ben More, I would be halfway back along the ridge when we would meet. No cardigan-clad, lay-by dwellers these. As far as I'm concerned anyone I meet out on the hills is a comrade and conversation would be more than welcome. Where had they been? Where were they going? Where were they staying? Had they found the caves?

I finished my hotel packed lunch, and set off back along the ridge to greet them. We met as predicted, halfway along. It was a couple in their thirties.

'Hello there,' I cried cheerfully from 15 feet away.

They didn't even look up as they stepped to one side to pass me, although the woman cast me one woeful backward look as they retreated.

To be charitable, perhaps they had been quarrelling about whether they would be able to see Schiehallion from the top. Maybe they'd come from a funeral, or had just discovered that there was to be another series of *Beadle's About*. To be uncharitable, perhaps they were just a pair of rude bastards, who should be slapped hard for not being polite enough to say hello to the only other human being for miles around.

It's always simple to find the path on the way down a hill, since you have the advantage of height, and so as I neatly avoided the boulder field I plodded down the track silently hoping that the couple had reached the summit of Ben More only to find they'd left their packed lunch in Perth.

On arriving back at the hotel I climbed into a bath and had a bit of a chat with myself before I lost the power of speech. At dinner I said 'thank you' three times, and 'Could I have a Becks please' once, before going to bed at 9.45.

If there's one thing lonelier than the wild hills of Scotland, it's the hotels.

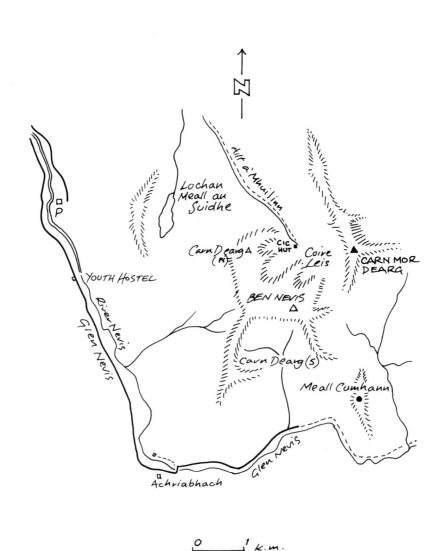

Carn Mor Dearg to Ben Nevis

Carn Mor Dearg; 1223m; (OS Sheet 41; 177722); M7.
Ben Nevis; 1344m; (OS Sheet 41; 166713); M1.

THE THOUGHT OF ASCENDING BEN NEVIS ON A SATURDAY FILLED ME WITH dread. Not because it is difficult. Far from it. People, for reasons best known to themselves, regularly push wardrobes or pull pianos up the motorway that calls itself the tourist path. The only technical difficulty therefore is getting past those carrying a flat-pack fitted kitchen, or getting stuck on the path blocked by a group descending with an attractive Liberty-print sofa bed and a nest of tables.

The feature that makes it dreadful is that it is crammed with unattractive tourists throughout the summer months, shambling around 50 feet above sea level in a state of exhaustion, asking everyone if they're near the top yet. Perhaps it's mountain snobbery to wish to avoid such a crowd, and if so then I am a mountain snob. It's precious meeting the odd soul on a high top and passing the time of day with them, knowing that no matter who or what they are, you share the same interests in wildlife, wilderness and solitude. It's quite another thing to share a summit with 60 people who express disappointment that there is no hot-dog stand.

However, if those who successfully gain the top, with or without the burden of living-room furniture, feel blessed with the exhilaration and wonder of their surroundings then I am happy for them, and glad they are able to share an emotion I regularly enjoy on the hills. It's merely that if there's more than 50 of them feeling it simultaneously on the same summit then I'd rather be somewhere else.

But the Ben must be bagged, and happily it can be combined with the ascent of another massive Munro, Carn Mor Dearg, which will steer you away from the tourist path and into some grander territory.

31

Rashly, I chose a Saturday in early summer to pick off the two peaks. The Ben is quite a different place in winter, equally as magnificent, but free from Pac-o-macs, folding aluminium chairs, and people who want to know who Benjamin Nevis was and why the mountain is named after him. But once you have unfolded an ordnance survey map and made the cheese and pickle sandwiches, it's hard to change your mind, and so on a hot June day I set off up the zig-zagging tourist path from Glen Nevis at ten o'clock in the morning.

The path was built to serve an observatory that functioned at the top of the Ben at the turn of the century. One trusts that its astronomers weren't quite the size of Patrick Moore or getting to work could have been problematic. Easy path or not, a climb of over 4,000 feet every Monday morning would certainly make me phone in with a headache. The track has been immaculately maintained considering the pounding it takes from trainers, brogues and sling-back stilettos, but being Britain's highest peak has elevated Ben Nevis above mere Munro status to major tourist attraction. A wooden bench a short way up strewn with cigarette ends tells you something about those who only make it that far, but then the path is a long, steep ascent for anyone unused to hill-walking.

To pass the heaving multitudes on the track, I raced up like a fell runner, unhappily only to find each time I successfully overtook what looked like a queue for an Andrew Lloyd Webber musical that there were further extensive crocodiles of people ahead. By this time I was frothing at the mouth like a rabid dog in walking boots with the effort of running in the heat, so I gave in and resumed normal speed.

There is no course of action that will help you lose the cacophony of teenagers yelling, adults whining and children screaming, until the turn off for Carn Mor Dearg, which joyfully appears at Lochan Meall an t-Suidhe. It's advisable therefore to assume a sociable demeanour and tolerate the company of your fellow man, rejoicing in his plain humanity all over the path. The nice beer-bellied English gentleman with the Union Jack T-shirt and shorts, a can of lager in one hand and a cigarette in the other, has just as much right to be there as you do. He probably thinks you're a plonker for carrying a rucksack and wearing hefty boots with gaiters when the temperature is in the eighties. So smile, be charming, and resist the temptation to elbow small children off the path to their doom for the crime of carrying a ghetto-blaster up the hill.

From the lochan you turn north-east, back into some semblance of peace.

A cairn marks the crossroads, and although the outrageously boggy path will cover you in peat to the armpits, you may hug yourself in delight to be walking in empty country again, as the cries of 'Look, Mam. Why is that man pushing a bed up the hill?' die behind you in the breeze.

However, beware of becoming overexcited that you are now on the path heading straight towards Carn Mor Dearg. It leads only to the Charles Inglis Clark mountain hut, a prestigious private hut owned by the Scottish Mountaineering Club and hence frequented by respectable rock-climbing doctors, lawyers and accountants. The hut is in a most peculiar situation, perched perfectly as the map would imply, to receive the maximum effect of the avalanche loading slopes behind it. Not only that, but one imagines such huts to be found in the very heart of the wilderness, where one cannot ascend a peak and walk out in a single day, and must take shelter for the night. Hardly the case here. A resident at the C.I.C. hut could easily do a spot of rock-climbing, nip into Fort William to indulge in some leisurely shopping for tartan gonks and still be back in time for a sing-song round the primus stove. Still, as long as the occupants are happy huddling in a spartan hut with the fantasy that they are men of the wilds, while people read the *Daily Record* under a golf umbrella and pass round the digestives a few thousand feet above them on the Ben then who can criticise? Each to their own.

So the path must be abandoned here while you strike down to cross the Allt a' Mhuilinn and start a relentless slog to attain the ridge of Carn Mor Dearg. From down in the corrie, the first view appears of the Ben's mighty cliffs and the spectacular Carn Mor Dearg Arête, which must be crossed to link the two peaks. Don't imagine you can walk easily straight up on to the Arête from the bottom of the corrie, as you may get into difficulties near the top unless you've a head for heights. It may look easy from the safety of the burn's heathery banks, but you would be wringing out your underpants if you found yourself clinging to near-vertical rock at the crest of the ridge by pursuing such a daft route. There are of course one or two ways up the face of the Arête but personally I wouldn't advise it. And you would miss Carn Mor Dearg which, after the relentless pull to climb on to its broad back, rewards you with the most fabulous views, and an easy walk to its summit. From here the cliffs of Ben Nevis are at their most dramatic, a sight sadly denied to those who take the tourist path. They approach the Ben from its wide whale-backed side, and hence stand at the top of these cliffs without being able to view them.

As you stroll or stumble along the ridge, you are presented with a vista of deep gullies, rarely without snow, and terrifying chimneys slicing up through the rock. To the east are the Aonachs, the brooding big beasts tamed to a degree now by poor old Aonach Mor's ski-tows, which it wears uncomfortably like a lorry driver sporting gold neck chains.

It's tricky, as someone who skis and mountaineers, to whine about the encroachment of ski developments in Scotland, especially when the developers of Aonach Mor spilt so much ink about how they were 'conservation friendly', they could have made a major motion picture out of their press releases. Unfortunately, all the bleating in the world about being green can't conceal the fact that a previously wild, virgin hillside now resembles Gateshead. They run the Gondola in the summer months too, which provides an additional worry that groups of sweet little old ladies in overcoats, support tights and patent shoes, could find themselves wandering aimlessly on top of a mountain over 4,000 feet high, without any concept of the dangers.

The next danger for me was the Arête. Carn Mor Dearg's cairn provides a perfect view of the remaining route, with the Arête sweeping elegantly off to the south-west. To those of us with vertigo, it fortunately reveals that the southern side of the ridge is not nearly as precipitous as the northern. This, in plain terms, means that apart from one small section of scrambling, you can chicken out and walk along the Arête with your head bobbing safely below the crest.

Constantly at war with my vertigo, I decided not to be pathetic and strode off on the flat, step-like slabs that top the crest of the ridge. After a spot of scrambling below the summit of Carn Mor Dearg, the only intimidating section is at the other end, just below the boulder field that will take you to the summit of the Ben.

Crampon marks on the ridge are a little disquieting. Not because you wonder if you need them in June, but because they are long white scars instead of neat little puncture marks. Call me suspicious, but this implies that the crampon, far from adhering steadily to the spot upon which its owner has chosen to commit his or her weight, has decided it prefers an altogether different rock and has gone for a bit of a slide. Written in stone all along the ridge therefore are visual records of people going 'Whoooaaargh!' with every step. This was not something upon which I wished to dwell, as I approached the narrowest section of the ridge. Being Saturday, there were a number of burly walkers picking their way over the granite from both directions which, unlike the presence of the bermuda-shorted brigade puffing their way up the other side of Ben Nevis, was curiously comforting.

As I gingerly stepped on to one last narrow slab, I met someone I knew walking the other way. Delightful as it was to meet pleasant company in such an unlikely place, I very badly wanted to exchange our felicitations on the other side of this rock. There, I felt, we could chat for hours without the fear of stepping back absentmindedly and continuing the conversation from a hospital bed in Fort William. He was having none of it, so I concealed my vertiginous anxieties.

We made some small talk as I tried to fix my eyes on his face to forget that my palms were sweating and my peripheral vision was registering only sky. The fact we were chatting about a programme on Radio 4 while standing on a dainty platform hundreds of feet tall seemed not to bother him. It was bothering me immensely. So I wrapped up the conversation as rudely as someone on *Newsnight* trying to silence a politician, just as he dealt me a social body blow. Would I mind taking his photo on this slab with the ridge spreading out behind him?

'Not at all,' said my mouth.

'LET ME OFF HERE!' screamed the rest of me.

So pressing his camera to my eye I tried to focus on this tanned, happy man, standing with one boot over the edge of a 200- or 300-foot drop, and the other on the edge of thin air. Who knows how the picture turned out? So prolific was my perspiration I steamed up the viewfinder, and I imagine my acquaintance now possesses a fine set of prints featuring the edge of my thumb and some clouds. We said our farewells and I leapt gratefully off the ridge and on to the safe path with the elegance of a stunned ox.

From here the last leg is a simple but muscle-tearing walk up a large boulder field to the summit of Ben Nevis. The posts stuck into the rock to your right as you ascend are markers for winter to stop people going off the edge; they also double as abseil posts for a quick escape route. There are those who think it rather offensive to erect such permanent climbing aids on a wild mountain, although we're not exactly talking a carved mahogany banister with brass handrails. It's also somewhat perverse to complain about a few innocent posts when the top of Ben Nevis is a lofty scrapyard.

Reaching the summit from the boulder field is a strange experience. From a steep ascent you emerge on to a surprisingly large plateau the

size of a football field, covered with cairns, memorial plaques, the ruined observatory, and of course the people you left behind on the tourist path. The ruins of the observatory are of interest but the rest of the summit could do with a hoover. But if you ignore the commemorative debris and assortment of international litter you will enjoy the most exhilarating views that can include over 100 Munros when visibility is good.

I arrived breathless, to find a large crowd and a respectable covering of snow on the summit. The snow in June was a revelation which seemed to astonish and dismay some girls in bikini-tops with a cold-box full of beer and a shoulder bag full of Jackie Collins novels, who had clearly hoped to picnic at the top. Britain's highest peak is not to be taken lightly. Although mountaineers will not need reminded, the less experienced need to be constantly alerted to the fact that a hot, sunny car park does not necessarily mean a benign hill-walk. The summit may be, and more often than not is, like Ice Station Zebra. Never feel uncomfortable warning people you encounter halfway up a mountain who are dressed for the beach that they are taking a great risk proceeding without extra clothing and food. You may sound like a Victorian headmaster, but how much worse would you feel to read of those people being injured, lost or

Fort William, Loch Linnhe and Loch Eil from Carn Mor Dearg

killed when you could have prevented it? So what if they tell you to sod off and mind your own business? At least your conscience will be clear.

Since nobody on the summit of the Ben required a ticking off, except perhaps by the fashion police, it was back on to the tourist path for the descent. Not only can you feel smug that you bagged the Ben the hard way, you will also be handsomely rewarded by the views across Loch Linnhe as you descend. Even depressed Fort William takes on a magnificence from this height as it glitters and reflects the late evening sun.

I avoided the mob on the path by descending 200 feet sledging on my rucksack on a long snow bank. I hasten to add before I am taken to court by mountain men with beards that this is highly irresponsible behaviour and extremely dangerous. Bloody good fun though. Safety pundits will be pleased to note that I received my just desserts that evening, on unpacking my rucksack and discovering that the action had mashed a forgotten egg sandwich into my hat.

The whole walk took in excess of nine hours, so not one to consider if you want to make it home in time for *Blind Date*. Don't let the volume of traffic discourage you from this superb walk. I was thrilled by it, delighted not only by the unsurpassed views in all directions, but by the physical challenge that a walk with so much climbing and descending presents. There is no denying that even in summer Ben Nevis is a magnificent peak, and a winter ascent for those well equipped and prepared will be a doubly stirring experience.

For those who wish to claim the peak with a selection of walnut dining-room furniture, try to avoid the hottest months of the year. Direct sunlight plays havoc with the varnish.

Rambler, Scrambler or Dangler?

I'VE ALWAYS SAID I CLIMB MUNROS. EVERYONE I GO CLIMBING MUNROS WITH says they climb Munros. We phone each other and say, 'Do you want to go and climb a Munro tomorrow?' It seems a logical thing to say if you fancy climbing a Munro, but apparently we are living a lie. We don't climb Munros because we are not climbers. Now you might think that a little strange, after all the *Concise Oxford Dictionary* defines 'climb' thus: 'ascend, mount, go up (often with help of hands)'.

Yep, that just about sums up what we do on the way to the cairn, hence the use of the word climb in trying to convey to a companion exactly what it is you expect them to do when they get out of the car. We don't say we writhe the Munros because we don't slither up them on our bellies, nor would we invite friends to hop, swim, float or jitterbug up a Munro on a Saturday. The term 'climb' has done us proud for years. The reason it is now unacceptable to say it is that at some point in recent history, rock-climbers held a secret annual general meeting and decided to keep the word to themselves. They climb, we merely walk.

Climbers also like to call themselves 'danglers'. This, I trust, has no connection with the fecal matter we are used to seeing hanging around the back end of a sheep, but instead refers to the fact they spend most of their weekends dangling from a rope.

The problem is that rock-climbers do all the hardest stuff in this game. Instead of meandering up a path to the top, chatting amicably to a pal about how George Michael used to be good in Wham and passing round the butterscotch, they choose a cliff and try to reach the summit by slowly inching their way up vertical rock, pushing their fingers into tiny fissures and standing with one toe on a ledge the size of a pebble. As you might imagine, this takes some time and is also completely mental. So on gaining the top, where the walkers are tucking into their second pork pie, the rock-climber needs some way to distinguish him or herself as greatly superior. This is hard. After all, the walkers got to the top first. The walkers have already had their lunch. The walkers still have some finger nails left and don't have skid marks in their boxer shorts. The rock-climber is powerless to inspire respect. But the revenge comes later in the pub.

Walker to rock-climber – 'So, were you out on the hill today?'

Rock-climber smiles sardonically, wiping his mouth with the back of a hairy arm. 'Yeah. Did an E7.'

Walker is confused. 'Oh. The Easains. Nice. A bit far away from Torridon though. Well we did Liathach. A lovely day's climb.'

Rock-climber chokes on beer. Splutters through ale-soaked beard. 'Climb? Climb did you say? You're talking walk in the park, matey! I mean I did a climb – A CLIMB! Comprende?'

Walker starts to regret starting conversation. Looks round for escape from this man who is obviously a few co-ordinates short of a bearing, and starts to back away slowly.

'Well, we certainly thought we were climbing, the wife and me, you know with all that pulling ourselves up over the rock and all, and what with the fact we were, well, in a manner of speaking, how can I put this, em, climbing up to the top.'

Rock-climber lunges at walker and tries to force-feed him his Yeti-gaiters until restrained.

A nasty, but not uncommon incident. So how can the simple walker make sure he avoids such an unpleasant confrontation with a dangler? Perhaps the most important lesson is to be able to recognise a rock-climber when you see one. Rock-climbers make sure they have lots of metal implements swinging from them at all times. This, I must confess, is quite sexy, in the same way that young, handsome joiners with their belt of tools strung low round their hips can make an impressionable adolescent girl want to have shelves erected. The rock-climber is held on a rope by clipping himself on to a harness thingy (if you've come to this book for technical information, boy are you going to be disappointed) that straps round his thighs and crotch, so as a quick guide to who the climbers are in the pub, just watch for those who seem to be constantly fiddling around in their genital area. I've noticed climbers do this a lot. They are always hitching up underpants, scratching away happily at unspeakable things in their breeches and, with one finger, boldly trying to free their underpants

that have become lodged somewhere dark and irretrievable that we can only guess at. Before any girls get excited at the prospect of all these crotch-obsessed men packing out Glencoe bars, and rush off to join a climbing club, I should point out they also smell like a circus tarpaulin and regard ten pints of Guinness as an aperitif.

So if we must accept that these climbers, or danglers, are kings of the mountains, then who comes next in this rigid pecking order? It's the scramblers. I, apparently, am a scrambler. That means that in addition to walking up the hill with my hands in my pockets, sometimes I scramble up rocks using my hands. Kind of obvious really. I can't imagine I would try and scramble up over rocks using my nose, but the use of hands in the mountaineering hierarchy seems to be of prime importance. Scramblers probably make up the majority of Munro-baggers, since to do them all you can't avoid scrambling, and will also be obliged to dangle once on the Inaccessible Pinnacle on Skye. There's noticeably less equipment hanging from a scrambler, but pound for pound there will be more fleecy material visible. Climbers like to break away from the usual uniform of breeches and warm top, favouring instead old tracksuit bottoms and rancid T-shirts, but the scrambler usually likes to be well turned out. However, the easiest way to distinguish the two groups is that the walker/scrambler will stand at the bottom of a difficult and dangerous mountain looking for a safe and easy way up, and the climber/dangler will stand at the foot of a safe and easy mountain looking for a difficult and dangerous way up.

Luckily for us scramblers, there is a group even further down the mountain social scale. They are known as ramblers. Unfortunately I am unable to advise you how to spot a rambler in a pub, since ramblers don't go into pubs. They either brew up tea on a little gas stove beside their car, or pop into a coffee house for a bun and a flick through *The Observer Book of Birds*. Ramblers are keen on things like 'rights of way', even though everywhere in Scotland is a right of way to those who cause no damage. This is because quite a lot of them are English and can't see the difference between Knoydart and Chipping Sudbury. They will write pamphlets and go on protest marches to keep open a path running from a new Barrett housing estate through a farmer's potato field to a scrap yard on the banks of a canal. They seem like terribly nice people, concerned with wildlife, erosion, litter and rights of way through potato fields, but a dangler or scrambler caught in a confined space with a tenacious rambler will end up either committing an act of violence or huddling in a foetal position in the corner, dribbling saliva from a defeated face as the rambler concludes his theory about red deer numbers.

Mountain Rescue get little trouble from ramblers, since their rambles rarely take them off a bus route, and you can sometimes spot them at the sides of the road, gazing into a hedgerow as their leader tells them a little about the history of couch grass.

Climbers make a great mistake, however, in imagining that each of these groups aspires to the dizzy heights of dangling. This is not true. I don't want to rock-climb. Unlike a sport like skiing, the considerable risks are not matched with sufficient exhilaration to kindle my interest, although I wouldn't say no if a boyfriend were to slip naked into one of those clanking climbing harnesses after a hot bath and a glass of wine.

Neither do ramblers wish to scramble. They are happy rooting around for Fly Agaric toadstools in a farmer's back garden until he sets the dogs on them, and would be miserable if you dragged them up anything taller than a caravan.

What is in dispute is who is allowed to say they went climbing. I shall carry on using the term regardless, and any hairy man who wants to challenge me about it is welcome to a wrestle. As long as he wears his harness.

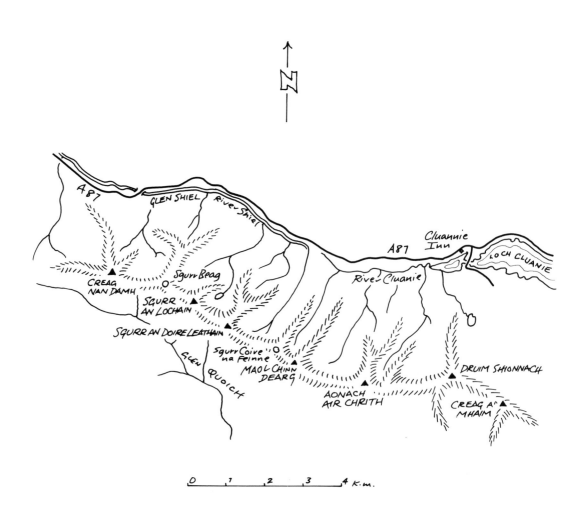

The South Glen Shiel Ridge

Creag a' Mhaim; 947m; (OS Sheet 33; 088078); M214.
Druim Shionnach; 987m; (OS Sheet 33; 074085); M155.
Aonach air Chrith; 1021m; (OS Sheet 33; 051083); M107.
Maol Chinn-dearg; 981m; (OS Sheet 33; 032088); M166.
Sgurr an Doire Leathain; 1010m; (OS Sheet 33; 015099); M116.
Sgurr an Lochain; 1004m; (OS Sheet 33; 005104); M126.
Creag nan Damh; 918m; (OS Sheet 33; 983112); M268.

EVEN THE MOST DEDICATED MUNROIST CAN BE SIDE-TRACKED BY THE WICKED pleasures of city life. The temptation to stay in town for a curry or a Schwarzenegger film, or both, can seriously disrupt that urge to carry on the journey up the 277 summits.

You can spot the symptoms of Munro fatigue immediately. Gradually a long lie on a Saturday comes to mean rising at 5 p.m. in time for the *Brookside* omnibus, your rucksack quietly grows grey mouldy bits at the back of a dark cupboard, and *The Face* seems more interesting than Tom Weir's 'My Month'. It's healthy, of course, to have more than one burning interest in life, but weekends are precious. To waste them cleaning out a drawer of plastic carrier bags instead of scrambling up lofty pinnacles is something you may regret. So should you discover that you are spending more time in Safeways than on the north-bound carriageway of the A9, it's time to tackle the South Glen Shiel Ridge.

In a single day, without leaving the ridge, a fit walker can pick off seven Munros and stagger back home to an orgy of peak-ticking at the back of the Munro book. There's no better inspiration for shrugging off slothfulness than Glen Shiel, which rewards with such a high score of tops and something worthwhile to brag about to those who spent Saturday and Sunday vacuuming the car with a cordless hoover.

The ideal place to start this heavenly 14-kilometre trek is from the equally lovely Cluanie Inn, a hotel at the western end of Loch Cluanie. I spent two nights there one summer, giving myself the immeasurable luxury of being able to start early from the hotel, still burping porridge and bacon, and return to a hot dinner, a steaming bath and a cosy bar full of fellow hill-walkers. You can camp nearby and use the Cluanie Inn for a hot bar-meal and somewhere to consume beer beside a log fire until they throw you out, but if you have the money why deny yourself a bed for the night?

The Cluanie Inn is a fine hotel in a splendid old building, which has been extended in recent years so sensitively, soon it will be difficult for passers-by to tell the old from the new. The new accommodation is on one floor, set round a pretty courtyard which echoes the traditional details of the existing structure. Of course this kind of thoughtful extension is alien to most Highland hotel owners. Their mission in life appears to be competing with one another in a race to remould their ancient and historic rural buildings into approximations of Birmingham town centre. If only such offenders were punished by having a Radio One DJ surgically joined to them at the hip, perhaps they would understand the crime of incongruous and pig-ugly extensions.

It's a stroke of great fortune that the Cluanie Inn's proprietors are more enlightened, since the building dominates the eastern end of the glen. As you wander along the ridge, it's a long time before you lose sight of its neat white contours, and if you take a strong pair of binoculars on your walk, you can keep an eye on how the housemaid is turning your bed down.

A long ridge-walk requires an early start, and a companion and I set off from the hotel at 8.30, toast crumbs still trembling on our lips, to attain the ridge by the first peak, Creag a' Mhaim. It's an easy walk up a tarmac estate road to the south-east of the hotel, which gently gains height until it's time to strike up the hillside towards Munro number one. There is no conspicuous path, but in fine weather the route could not be more obvious.

I had looked forward to a leisurely ramble amongst the hills, since we had started early and the days were long. But as we left the tarmac road and headed up the hill I made a grave error. We came across a small party of people sitting innocently on a rock enjoying the sunshine. Obviously they had risen even earlier. They said hello cheerily as we passed, and for no particular reason other than mindless banter I concluded our exchange with some hopeless attempt at humour, which happily has been blacked from my memory. I recall the gist of it implied that they couldn't sit there sunbathing too long if they wanted to get through all seven tops. Not exactly side-splitting, but not grounds for assault either, one would think. One of the men bristled visibly as the others smiled their pleasant responses. The race was on.

Although ten full minutes passed after leaving his party swigging juice happily and pointing at the loch, a casual glance backwards revealed that they were gaining on us quickly. This was very strange. To have closed such a gap the niggled gentleman must have swiped the juice from his companions' lips the moment we passed and kick-started them into a sprint. It may be a childish response, but when you have overtaken someone on a hill, it is very uncomfortable to be overtaken by them. We stepped up the pace. So did they.

The ridge is quickly gained and on this peach of a day was absolutely magnificent, with the hills retaining sizeable patches of spring snow that sparkled in the hazy sunshine. Although there are no technical difficulties on this walk, the ridge rarely disappoints, and the terrain varies from narrow, dramatic sections that thrill with their mantle of cliffs, to huge grassy plains pitted with tiny alpine flowers.

The ridge presents its craggy face to the north and rolls away in steep, but somewhat tamer, banks to the south. Unlike a ridge like the Aonach Eagach where escape is impossible until the end, it is not only feasible, but very tempting to come off the ridge and wander into the wild land of the Glenquoich forest that appears so inviting from the tops. On a summer's day, the sun glitters on Loch Quoich, back-lighting the lonely bridge that takes a single track road to the remote Kinloch Hourn. You can just make it out as you cross from Aonach air Chrith to Maol Chinn-dearg, with Loch Quoich sparkling behind Gleouraich, another fabulous mountain.

Slicing through Gleouraich's slopes are some incredibly well-constructed stalkers' paths. My heart sank when I first viewed them, since huge paths marching across wild hills usually signal the coming of insensitive forestry. But I was comforted to discover that these highways are antiquities, built by some unfortunate landowner who expected a visit from the king. The king never turned up and the laird was left with paths on which he could hold a formula one race. I say unfortunate laird, but of course it would have

OVERLEAF:
Looking east along the
South Glen Shiel Ridge

47

been the unfortunate estate workers who would have hauled the pick-axes up the hill and toiled away for weeks, just so that somebody with a crown could sit on a pony that didn't stumble on his way up a mountain to shoot something. Hard to feel sorry for the laird, who would have watched the sweating workers from his window, hands in pockets, listening for the doorbell in case the king changed his mind and dropped in for a scone.

We completed the first four Munros with relative ease, since there is little rising or dropping between peaks, and cruised along a gloriously flat section of the ridge having fantasies about lunch. There were a number of walkers now, all taking their time and drinking in the view, but the chap at our heels had now resorted to breaking away from his party to try and close the gap so obviously gnawing at his soul. I had never done anything as crass as race on a hill-walk before, but it was starting to amuse. Although it hardly seemed fair racing a man at least 15 years our senior, who could resist going just a little faster every time we saw his face contorted with exertion, glaring up at us like Charles Laughton in *Mutiny On The Bounty*?

A lunch break would give him his chance, forcing him to make a decision whether or not to delay his own sustenance in order to overtake us as we crammed fruit cake into our faces. We decided to halt the nonsense and stopped for a sandwich on a picturesque rocky outcrop that provided views east and west along the glen, and over to spectacular Knoydart. The running man took his opportunity, and as he passed, followed by his less competitive, wheezing companions, clearly suffering agonies by his pace-setting, he gave us a triumphant, knowing nod.

What is more enjoyable than silently consuming chicken sandwiches surrounded by scenery that immobilises any other emotion but wonder? Once gained, the ridge never disappoints. The best route is east to west, as following the sun results in the treat of trying to glimpse the sea and watching the sun set. It brings a hazard too. Even though the wind kept the tops cool, the sun was relentless, and I foolishly changed out of my breeches into shorts for the remainder of the route. I wonder when I will learn that on a long walk in a single unchanging direction, one will automatically go home with a left leg sporting first-degree burns and a right limb like a piece of white Italian veal? However, elation at the beauty of the surroundings meant tandooried legs were far from my thoughts, and as we continued to the shapely Sgurr an Lochain, towering as it does over a tiny dark blue lochan, we agreed it couldn't get much better.

Although there is no mention of it on the map, I could swear that the

tiny loch has a crannog in it. I'm sure archaeologists will rush to correct me but, from the vantage point high above it, there does seem to be a suggestion of a circular structure beneath the water, joined to the banks by a walkway. If it is a crannog, it's in a strange place, stuck high above the glen in a corrie. It would have taken its occupants hours to get to the Cluanie Inn for a pint from there.

Just as we stepped over a rise, we nearly fell over the boy racer and party having their lunch. The others acknowledged us cheerily, clearly relieved to have been allowed 30 seconds for a sit-down. He looked catatonic with rage. As we parted, we could hear our man force-feeding his companions their scotch eggs, hurrying them along like a rowing cox.

He didn't catch us until the last peak, Creag nan Damh, where a number of ridge-walkers were gathered, basking in the delight of the afternoon and resting on their laurels after a mammoth expedition. If you had any energy at all, you could keep height and continue to Sgurr na Sgine and on to The Saddle, but you would need thighs like Graeme Souness's. It's here you come to realise three things. 1. The South Glen Shiel Ridge is fabulous. 2. You have seven miles to walk back to the hotel as you haven't got two cars. 3. You're knackered. Very gingerly, everybody started to question each other about transport. No, nobody had left a car at the bottom of this hill, and, yes, everybody was looking to cadge a lift.

OVERLEAF:
Looking west along the
South Glen Shiel Ridge

51

By this time our pursuer had joined the merry band on the peak, and we could hear his companions gasping not far behind him. We had beaten him, but he played a final trump card. He had two cars. They were at the bottom of the hill. He was going back to the Cluanie Inn. Yes, there was probably room for us all.

Normally, walking along tarmac is a piece of cake after the rocky excursion along a ridge. But in summer the A87 is crammed with caravan-dragging buffoons who drive as though wearing strait-jackets. The choice for the pedestrian is either a leap into the ditch for safety, or a nasty death smeared over their ridiculous tin box like a dripping red caravan-club sticker. There was nothing else for it. It was time to give in and do a bit of grovelling.

All the way down we listened with feigned interest to our man's proud record of clock-beating on other hills. We tolerated his hilarious English mispronunciations of the Scottish hills that had taken him less than three hours, keeping in mind the thought of that comfortable car seat at the bottom of this rough heather slope every time we felt like killing him. At

Looking south towards Loch Quoich

last we arrived at his car, where several other walkers were hanging around looking dolefully along the road.

I couldn't do it. I just couldn't take a journey in a confined space with a man who pronounced Sgurr na Ciste Duibhe as Sisty Dub and didn't think it was as good as the Lake District.

Just as this realisation dawned, a luckless couple drew into the parking space to read a map. Before they knew what was happening we had opened their door, asked for a lift, said thank you and got in. A good tip in hitching is to approach your intended lift when stationary. It's practically impossible to say no to someone who's actually loaded their rucksack into your boot and clipped on their seatbelt. With little choice they drove us sullenly to the hotel. As you drive, or walk, God forbid, back along the road, it's hard to believe you have travelled all that way at a lofty 3,000 feet. The ridge seems massive from the road, and when we tried to tell our driver where we'd been, he grunted in disbelief. Well it may have been a grunt of irritation that his lovely hire-car was steaming up with two sweaty, stinking hill-walkers who had forced their way in uninvited, but I prefer to think disbelief.

The cold pint at the Cluanie Inn was nectar and, as we polished it off, our man and his party arrived. Not only had we beaten him on the ridge, but without cars we had unwittingly beaten him back to the hotel. The walkers who had wangled the lift with him looked as if they had been told they had a week to live, suggesting the car conversation must have fulfilled my expectations.

We bought him and his friends a drink which gave him a chance to quiz us on our movements for the next day. My companion's eyes glittered impishly as he said we would be combining The Five Sisters with The Saddle and Sgurr na Sgine, hoping to be finished by 5 p.m.

'It'll take an early start,' he said.

We retired to a hot bath and glimpsed them only briefly over a sweet trolley later at dinner. The next morning was drizzling, damp and miserable and our man and his party were not at breakfast.

'You're not first up this morning,' said the waiter. 'That other lot left at 6.30 to do The Five Sisters and The Saddle.'

We ate a leisurely breakfast and then drove to Skye to have some scones.

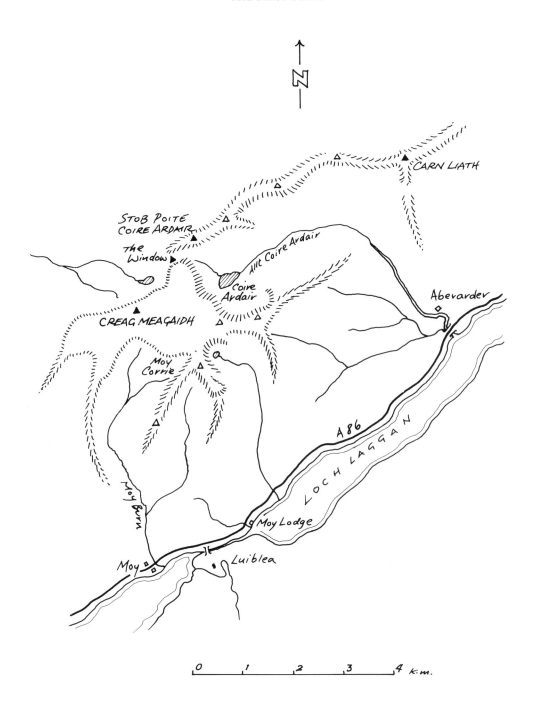

Creag Meagaidh

Creag Meagaidh; 1130m; (OS Sheets 34 and 42; 418875); M26.

SOMETIMES EVEN THE EASIEST OF MOUNTAINS CAN DEFEAT YOU. THERE IS nothing particularly difficult about Creag Meagaidh, unless it comes up in a spelling test, yet it took me three attempts to get to the top of the damned thing.

It's only in recent years that I've learned to use the weather forecast before contemplating a hill-walk. Millions of pounds spent on satellite technology is wasted when people like me ignore Michael Fish yelling on television from behind some sandbags, 'For God's sake take cover!' as we set off to claim a Munro with a song in our hearts.

It was just such foolhardy behaviour that enabled me continually to miss the summit of Creag Meagaidh. The first attempt was in winter, precisely at that dark, depressing period when the sun can barely be bothered rising for more than 20 minutes before it packs in and hands over to nightfall. The weather on this occasion seemed ideal. A heavy snowfall left the hills deliciously inviting and the sky was clear and bright.

Two of us set off up the long path from Aberarder at the mind-bogglingly stupid time of 11.30 a.m. In the mists of time I cannot recall why we started so late. Perhaps there was a party the night before, maybe we hung around in bed too long doing moist wicked things, or more likely I just slept in. Whatever the excuse, we reached Lochan a' Choire at 3 p.m. when the sun was starting to remember it was needed elsewhere. Simple arithmetic told us that even if we gained the summit we would be stumbling back down in the dark like late cinema-goers trying to find their seats.

As we sat at the loch eating a cold lunch, deciding who could first pin the blame on the other for messing up the day, we heard voices from the cliffs surrounding the lochan. A third of the way up a vicious-looking ice-climb were two men, slowly hacking an unenviable route with axes and crampons. By this time it was past 3.30, the light was fading fast, and the blizzard that the ignored weatherman had warned would sweep the Highlands was whipping into action. That's odd, we thought. Perhaps they're going to spend the night on the mountain. Maybe they're top mountaineers training for a Himalayan expedition that requires constant overnight bivvying on icy rock faces. So we ignored them and went home. Unfortunately they turned out to be two fools who didn't realise the time, and brought Mountain Rescue out combing the hill for them next morning. Luckily, they had survival gear and were found alive and well, albeit a trifle sheepish, at the top of the climb.

I felt rather guilty after that episode. When should you tell Mountain Rescue that you think there might be somebody in danger? After all, if those two boys had died, it would have been on our consciences that we saw them get into difficulty and did nothing. On the other hand, imagine the embarrassment of calling a full-scale search out for somebody who is not only not in peril, but is mightily cheesed off to be awoken from a deep sleep by an RAF Sea-King helicopter blowing the filling out of their sleeping-bag? Not to mention the danger you put the members of the Mountain Rescue team in by expecting them to stagger about in the snow with sticks when they should be back home with their slippers on watching *McGregor's Scotland*.

I feel the same way about the police. When two men tried to break into my kitchen via a skylight window at midnight while I was at home, I made the grave error of dialling 999. Not only did the street fill with sirens and blue lights like an episode of *Kojak*, the cops that piled up the stairs were too fat to get through the attic space and pursue the men. That left me with dozens of portly gentlemen in blue who spent the rest of the night eating my shortbread, drinking my coffee and asking me if I knew Terry Wogan. Next time I will simply invite the burglars in. I'm certain they at least would refuse a second slice of cake.

Even though the plight of those two climbers should have released me from my fear of calling for help on behalf of others, I'm still wary unless I come across someone whose legs are a few hundred yards from their body. Reminding others that they don't have much light left, or are not equipped for the top, is quite different. But I live in fear of calling out the rescue team for a solitary figure glimpsed high on a darkening summit, only to find it's Hamish McInnes nipping back up to fetch a dropped mitten.

That was the first attempt at Creag Meagaidh. The second, on a blustery Sunday in October, was more frustrating. Ignoring the weather forecast yet again, a number of us packed our rucksacks and headed up that interminable path to Coire Ardair. Meanwhile, canny Munroists who paid attention to satellite technology, which indicated a depression deeper than Christmas in Barlinnie, were sitting at home by the fire eating cheese on toast. We should have taken some heed from the birch trees half way up the track which were bending double in the gale, and from the fact that five minutes after leaving the car, we were wetter than the Scottish Sub-Aqua team. This, however, was a determined pack and we were not going to be put off by small obstacles like being unable to stand up or walk forward. This time I at least got past the lochan and up on to the boulder field that leads to the window. The window is a coll neatly dividing Creag Meagaidh and another Munro, Stob Poite Coire Ardair but, more significantly, it acts as a highly efficient wind tunnel. As we lurched up the soaking, slimy boulders towards it, like a team of wet-look mime artists walking against the wind, one of our party stopped and said, 'Let's go back.'

At least we all hoped that's what he said. In the gale it sounded like, 'Ehh . . . oaaah . . . aaaack.'

We were back in the car with the heater on before you could say 'Who finished the soup?' and another attempt was foiled.

The last failure was human. I made the mistake of telling two non-hill-walking friends that they could easily manage Creag Meagaidh. The day was perfect. A crisp winter morning greeted us with snow quilted in twinkling ice crystals. The time was 9 a.m., the sky was clear and blue, and nothing was going to stop me this time. What I failed to realise was that to those who never walk up mountains, visiting the bank, the post office and the dry cleaners on the same day is considered a triathlon.

My friends had to have their first sit-down in sight of the car. I was heartbroken. By 12.30 we had just made the birch wood and had to admit defeat. Friendship is more important than mountaineering, and so for their sakes I told them they'd done very well and we turned back to the prospect of a more leisurely Sunday afternoon, with colour supplements, cats, coffee and carpets to lie on. I cast one longing glance up at the cliffs of Coire Ardair, where the sun was glancing off the icy tips of gleaming rock, and I knew that next time I'd get the sucker.

It was therefore with a fit companion that I tackled the brute for a

OVERLEAF:
Looking east along
Loch Laggan

59

*The Window, Creag
Meagaidh*

fourth attempt. This time we planned to take in two other Munros on the northern ridge of the corrie, Carn Liath and Stob Poite Coire Ardair, before dropping down to the window and back up on to Creag Meagaidh's vast plateau.

It was an amazing frosty morning, with a strange, silent mist hanging only a few hundred feet high. My heart sank at the prospect of yet again missing the top in the thick fog, but we had a great treat in store. We left the path, shrouded in a beautiful and eerie veil of mist, coloured pink with the rising sun, and clambered up the hillside towards the ridge of Cairn Liath. My friend was about 50 feet above me and almost out of sight in the fog, when I heard him yell at me to 'come and see this'. Those who have never been up a mountain when temperature inversion is at work have missed the most splendid sight. We were standing above the clouds, which formed a thick, bulbous ocean at our feet, out of which in every direction rose mountain tops like islands. The mist was breaking against the peaks like waves, the sun was radiant in a perfectly clear blue sky above us, and I was awe-struck. Ahead of us we could see our ridge, standing clear of the cloud, brushed purple in the strange early light. The ridge-walk was one of the most wonderful I can recall, as the sea of cloud broke up

only on gaining the Creag Meagaidh plateau, and the day remained crystal clear until the last.

On the ridge, above the clouds

Some may find the summit of Creag Meagaidh a little disappointing after the drama of its cliffs and corrie. The top is not visible from the road, and were it not for a sizeable cairn you could miss it altogether. The plateau is huge, flat and featureless, and tests the map-reading ability of those who arrive in anything but perfect visibility. A common error is to think that the large cairn first encountered when gaining the plateau from the window is the true summit. It is in fact something called Mad Meg's Cairn and nobody knows what the hell it's doing there. The Nature Conservatory Council, who thankfully own Creag Meagaidh, have a couple of suggestions, including it being a monument to a lost lover or an old protection for a rowan tree. Gardeners amongst you will doubtless argue that piling a ton and a half of rubble on top of your sapling is a somewhat off-beat method of protection, so I'll take the old lost love yarn, thanks.

I'm pleased the NCC bought the mountain, since a commercial forestry firm had plans to cover the whole area in vile rows of sitka spruces to help chat-show hosts and snooker players in England make a killing on their tax is a life-style statement. Every shop selling rucksacks displays dazzling coloured examples in every size and shape. And yet out on the hill there are still people walking around with dark-green self-coloured rucksacks. It must take enormous strength of character to fly in the face of peppermint green, fuchsia and sunshine-yellow rucksacks, and actually sign the cheque for one in dark green. I take my hat off to such people, although I wouldn't like to spend a night in a bothy with them.

Having chosen the sack, it's time to decide how to wear it, and what to have hanging from it. The things that swing from your rucksack are as important as what rides inside. Climbers show the world they are more than just pansy hill-walkers by covering their rucksacks with ropes, metal things and more metal things. A keen hill-walker will have an ice-axe and crampons dangling from their rucksack for most of the year (until somebody in Raybans, shorts and a T-shirt laughs at them), and it's important how and where you attach this ice-axe, since an inexpertly dangled implement can end up swinging loose into your bottom with alarming momentum. Most good rucksacks will have special loops to fit the axe, but if, like me, your rucksack was designed in 1952 to take some quail's eggs and a pair of gloves, then you will end up being creative with the straps. The worst thing you can do is to attach the shaft of the ice-axe to something stable and the pick end of it to something that may give way. That's a recipe for Mountain Rescue turning up to find you impaled to a memorial cairn in the most unbecoming fashion. The best policy is to carry it like a walking stick. If it's cold and icy enough to need one, then you should have it out all the time anyway, but it does rather leave you wondering what else you can hang from the rucksack. Try animal skulls. At least you'll get a space to yourself at the cairn.

Packing the rucksack is an art, and a friend of mine always packs his to capacity, even on a two-hour walk. He takes a complete change of clothing, a sleeping-bag and ground mat, food for two days, a head torch, compass, spare laces and a small stove for emergency cooking. This may seem excessive, but then this was a man who through a grave time miscalculation, became 'be-nighted' on Liatach. His frequency in recounting the tale of being 'be-nighted' prompted his friends to call him Sir Peter. This is a cautionary tale in the use of mountain-speak. Never say 'be-nighted' – just say you got caught overnight on the hill. However, Sir Peter will want for nothing if it happens to him again, since he carries more creature comforts in his rucksack than I have in my house.

So if you have time to spare, remember that the packing and stocking of the rucksack is all-important in preparing for that expedition into the hills. Slothfulness may overwhelm you, and you may want to stay up and watch a Chilean film on Channel 4 until two in the morning, but believe me you will regret it the next day if that rucksack is still unpacked and neglected.

There is, of course, a general rule you can follow to ensure that your rucksack is always well stocked, ready for action, with delicious sandwiches packed in Tupperware boxes, clean and tidy, and with no nasty surprises lurking in any of the pockets. Marry someone rich and get Filipino help.

Filming the Munros

IT'S A MISTAKE TO FOLLOW MY ADVICE, FOR THE SIMPLE REASON THAT
I never follow it myself. When a young TV researcher I was working
with asked me which sort of programme they should work on next, I
furrowed my brow, leant over and wagged a finger. 'Never . . .' I said
sagely, fixing their astonished gaze, '. . . never, ever work on a programme
about something you love doing in your spare time. You will grow to
loathe your own hobby.'

A year later I was heaving myself up An Teallach with a film crew,
making *The Munro Show* for Scottish Television.

So I was wrong. Filming the Munros didn't make me hate them, but it
did give me the opportunity to nearly wipe out a team of six people.

It started when I foolishly mentioned to Alastair Moffat at Scottish that
I was in the middle of writing a book about Munros. He was looking for
an outdoor series, and since I was already bathed in the sweat of mountain
fever I rashly suggested putting together a programme based on some of
the subjects I had been scribbling about. This was not a particularly sensible
idea at the time. There were very good reasons why nobody had done a
regular, magazine-format hill-walking programme before, not least the fact
that film crews can rarely be persuaded to walk more than 50 yards from
their car, and start to whine and paw the director if they can't break for
a pub lunch at 1 p.m. sharp. I was going to have to ask a crew to strap
equipment to their backs, climb 12 mountains over 3,000 feet, and think
themselves lucky if they managed a ten-minute break for a sandwich at
the top.

Far be it from me to mention that there had been certain other pro-
grammes where some cheating had gone on, by flying film crews to the
tops of hills in helicopters and pretending they had hoofed it. This certainly
would not do for *The Munro Show*. Not just because of the underhand

169

deception, but because to spend the latter part of the summer out walking the hills and be paid for it seemed too good a chance to miss. We knew we would have to use a helicopter to get high dramatic shots to cut in with the bulk of the programme, but everyone agreed the only way to make it work would be to climb the mountains first, in exactly the way a normal hill-walker would.

Assembling the crew was like asking for volunteers to join a chain gang, yet we had everybody in under a week. Alasdair Walker, the cameraman, was already a keen hill-walker, sound man Brian Howell wasn't but was keen to try, Ross Murray, the researcher, was a bearded rock-climber who had done well over 100 Munros, Angus Lamont, the associate producer, said he didn't mind a standard ten-hour day in the wilds, although he rolled his eyes when he said it, and Vivien Robertson, the production manager, who would normally expect to be in a cosy office with a fan heater under the desk, found herself heaving camera batteries up mountains before she could get to a phone and call her union. With three willing, interchangeable runners, Rod, Ronnie and Fraser, the mountain team was complete.

When you have a crew that will go anywhere, the opportunities are huge, and so we chose the hardest and most dramatic hills we could think of to make the series spectacular. The problem was we couldn't start filming until halfway through August. Any hill-walker knows that not only does the weather start to deteriorate precisely at this time, but the men with rifles are polishing their barrels and dusting down their plus fours for the impending deer-stalking season. Not a great time to start a series about mountains, but we had no choice. How was I to know we would come a cropper on a fairly regular basis? My lawyers are working on some plausible excuses.

THE AONACH EAGACH

At least we started filming without too many traumas, other than blisters the size of fried eggs on the long walk back out of Creag Meagaidh, but when the stalking season got underway we were struggling with access problems. So in mid-September we headed for Glencoe to do the Aonach Eagach ridge, since The National Trust For Scotland who own it allow access all year round. It's almost worth buying one of their bookmarks with baby owls on them at their visitor centre, just to say thank you. No, come to think of it, that's asking a bit too much. On arrival, however, Glencoe was under a characteristic downpour. Our hearts sank. The weather forecast said the West of Scotland should have cleared by 10 a.m., but nobody had told Glencoe. We hung around miserably in the Clachaig eating gargantuan quantities of cheese toasties until we felt sick. In such situations everybody tries to look busy. Vivien always has calls to make, Ali and Brian can fiddle with screwdrivers and lens cloths, and I try and look like a producer doing some work by opening my big folder and laying it out on the table. Nobody is ever fooled by this device, since all I do is put my coffee on top of it and stare vacantly into space for two hours. Then suddenly, at noon the clouds began to lift.

Making a programme up a mountain is quite different to hill-walking for fun. Every time I decide I want to say something to camera it takes on average half an hour to get all the equipment out, perform the piece and then pack it all back up again. If I'm in usual form, which means 15 takes just to remember which mountain we're on, then it can take considerably longer. So knowing that we couldn't possibly start and finish the ridge in so short a time with those difficulties in mind, it was agreed that a walk to the top of Am Bodach would do for the day. We would have to come back and complete the ridge when the weather improved. At least that was the plan. Sunset was at 8.30 p.m. that day and it seemed like a long way off.

At 2 p.m. we started up the steep path to Am Bodach at the east end of the ridge. Ali Walker had purchased a rucksack that would take the awkward bulk of his camera, and although it weighed more than any of us would care to carry across a room without having to sit down, he was always miles ahead on every walk. This, quite naturally, was a source of some irritation. Every other outdoor programme appears to make a big deal of how 'the crew are carrying such heavy equipment, they'll be continuing by Land-Rover while we walk over the top and meet them'. So it was rather annoying when the crew carrying the heavy stuff kept a constant 20 yards in front of the presenter carrying only her sandwiches and a hat. I resolved to give them all a bit of a talking to later, but the weather was spectacular by the time I caught up with Ali to do the first link, at a dramatic spur of rock called The Chancellor. The views down Glencoe from here are fabulous, and after a morning of torrential rain, with a cloud level of about four feet, the glistening sunlit rocks on Bidean Nam Bian, the warmth of the sun and the azure blue sky acted on our spirits like a drug. It's this elated part of the day I blame for what happened later. We carried on up to Am Bodach, where the vista across to Ben Nevis and the Mamores was breathtaking. We stopped and had a conference about what to do.

OVERLEAF:
Rannoch Moor from
Buachaillie Etive Mor

171

The Aonach Eagach is mainland Britain's narrowest ridge, a walk between two Munros, Meall Dearg and Sgorr Nam Fiannaidh, and for someone like me who suffers from vertigo, it's a brown underpants job.

If doing the walk from east to west, it's at Am Bodach you have to make the decision to go down or carry right along to the end, since once on the ridge there's no way off until you reach the second Munro. Researcher Ross looked at his watch and said we'd never make it now, and we should probably go back. But the sun was beating down, the visibility was incredible and the hills of Scotland had never looked more beautiful. We all shouted at him in derision and decided to carry on, but Ross was not a happy man.

The first bit of scrambling occurs just after Am Bodach, and takes you up to Meall Dearg. It was horrible. However, nobody else seemed to be suffering, and every time I looked round for support they were chatting to each other with their hands in their pockets about whether we should stop off later for a curry in Fort William. I started to feel a little hard done by. Others could get away with being frightened in privacy, whereas my yellow streak was to be recorded for a few million people to share and snigger at. We carried on to the narrowest section of the ridge, where some careful navigation round a pinnacle is required to reach the safety of a wider path and where the feeling of exposure is tremendous. I wanted this filmed as it happened, so the crew crossed first and set up, leaving me behind to climb across towards them when they were ready. So cowardly was I, however, that I made Ross hide behind bits of rock just in front of me, to whisper where I should put my feet. Pathetic I know, but you have no idea how comforting it is having someone with a beard in front of you hissing, 'Psst . . . foothold to the left!'

The trouble is that all this trauma took a great deal of time, even though we were practically running between the scrambling sections, and by the time we reached the second Munro it was 8 p.m.

The sun was setting over the sea and I have never seen anything so spectacular. Ali the cameraman agreed, and while Ross danced around, frothing at the mouth and pointing at his watch, we were taking shot after shot of the mountains fading through purples and pinks into a glorious dusk. Mountaineers among you will quickly deduce that if we were filming the sun setting from the last Munro, it would have gone completely by the time we were ready to descend. You would be right. We had planned to come down safely on the north side of the ridge, beside the pap of Glencoe, but

OVERLEAF:
The film crew. From
left to right: Angus
Lamont, Vivien
Robertson, the author
and Alasdair Walker.
Crouching: Brian
Howell and Ross
Murray

175

after a hurried conference we decided to attempt a descent by the terrifying path above the Clachaig which the Scottish Mountaineering Club book strongly advises against, even in daylight. It would save us valuable time, and although dangerous the general opinion was that stumbling down the heathery slopes to the north in the dark, without benefit of a clear path, would mean a broken leg every hundred yards.

It was totally dark when we gained the upper reaches of the path, and I buckle under the embarrassment that not one of us had a head torch. Never, under any circumstances, attempt to descend that path in the dark. In fact, never under any circumstances attempt to descend it at all. Every rock is loose, and the gradient is so severe that the lights of the Clachaig could be seen between our feet as we stumbled down like toddlers looking for their mum. We were totally silent as we picked a way through the black night, with the sounds of revelry in the bar below drifting up to us, torturing us in our plight. Each step knocked another boulder down into the inky abyss below and possibly on to somebody's head, and there was little energy left to deal with this last and most dangerous hurdle. Everyone was practically dead on their feet, and apart from the regular shouts of 'below!' and 'aaaargh . . . a rock!' only Ross had enough energy to say anything, which was a series of variations on 'I told you so'. It was so dark nobody could see each other, and we could only trust we still had a complete party by the sounds of people whimpering nearby. The only way to navigate was by the luminescence of white rocks on the path.

We burst into the Clachaig at 10.30 p.m., just as the manager's fingers twitched on the phone dial to call out Mountain Rescue. Imagine how humiliating it would have been to have a rescue team come and fetch a film crew making a programme about how to tackle the Munros. We muttered about why we were so late and stuck our red and sheepish faces into some beer glasses to consume the most welcome pints imaginable. It was a miracle nobody was hurt and I resolved it would never happen again. Well at least that was the best-laid plan, but you know what Burns said about those.

THE IN PIN

Skye is not exactly famous for a Mediterranean climate, so I can't imagine why we were surprised to find it cold, wet and miserable on arrival. We had come to film the ultimate Munro, Sgurr Dearg, known to those who quake in their walking boots at the thought of rock-climbing as the Inaccessible Pinnacle, but it's not a task that can be contemplated in high winds and torrential rain. At this point in the shoot we were so familiar with the weather forecast that we shouted about isobars and depressions in our sleep, but the tiny regional variations can make the difference between being able to climb and film, or not being able to get out of the car.

The Met Office promised two clear days and we planned an early start to take advantage of them the very next day. After our Aonach Eagach experience, we had invested in head torches and made a strict rule about when we should leave the summit. This was later still in the season, and sunset was around 7.30, so Ross demanded assurance that we would leave no later than 6 p.m. from the base of the In Pin to make our descent. It was a deal. Nobody wanted another night hike. We set off early from the Glen Brittle Memorial hut and made good progress up on to the ridge that leads to Sgurr Dearg. It was slightly overcast, but the cloud level was high above the peaks and there was no wind, so the only worry for me was whether I would see my breakfast again when I stood in front of the climb. Although Sgurr Dearg is not a particularly high Munro, at only 986 metres, the going is tough and I was puggled as well as petrified when at last we stood beneath that terrifying blade of rock that is the In Pin.

We were to be disappointed. From nowhere, a mist swirled in and obscured the summit, but more perilously, left the rock too wet and slippery to climb safely. The more usual way to the top for Munroists is by the long sloping fin of the rock on its westerly side, where the ascent is no more than an exposed scramble. But we were going for a climb up the vertical eastern face for two reasons. Firstly, that it would make better TV, and secondly Ross pointed out that for a first-time rock-climber like me, it was safer to be on a vertical climb where a fall would mean a dangle straight down on a few feet of tight rope, instead of a huge, dangerous pendulum swung over the longer side. I suspected the real reason was Ross wanting vengeance for an entire summer of jokes about his beard, but I kept my fears to myself.

With the summit still in cloud at 5.30, the day was useless and we skulked off down to a horrible dinner in a grim Skye hotel. We had a rule that we didn't climb two days in a row, to save people's leg muscles and stop a full-scale mutiny erupting. But we awoke the next day to the news that the weather was going to improve from early afternoon, so we broke our own code and headed back up the mountain to have another go.

Looking out to the Inner Hebrides

Sgurr Alasdair and the Great Stone Shoot

All the way up the sun shone and light clouds scurried across the sky. From the ridge the walker can look across Coire Lagan and see the magnificent scree slopes of mighty Sgurr Alasdair, a sight that requires the viewer to plunder their own thesaurus for adjectives to describe its beauty. Coire Lagan is a wonderful sight as it cradles a blue-green lochan in its arms and is ringed by ferocious grey cliffs, and the scale of Sgurr Alasdair perceived from high above the corrie on the Sgurr Dearg ridge is unnerving. The ridge also offers views across the sea to the islands of Rhum, Eigg, Canna and Soay, and it was notable that climbing it a second day made none of these features any less enthralling.

The Cuillins of Skye are quite unlike anywhere else in Scotland, and depending on the weather they appear as if part of a desperate barren moonscape or take on an Alpine grandeur. They couldn't quite make up their mind that day, and swung from being dark and demonic one moment, to sunlit and genial the next. When we arrived at the base of the In Pin, with the second day's climb taking its toll on energy and good humour, the summit was clear. Unfortunately a party of climbers were in the process of making their way to the top along the long southerly side, so we were required to wait for them to complete their climb and abseil down. My nerves were on edge as I realised that it had to be today or never. Would it be easy like Ross said? Would I fall off and die? Could I make the abseil down without crying? At least I was going to see some people doing it properly before we had to give it a go. That, I was sure, would put my mind at ease.

Half an hour later we were watching with our mouths open as a girl on the summit was lowered down from the top on a rope like a sack of potatoes, whacking her face against the rock as her hands were busy high above her head holding on to her lifeline. Cruelly hilarious as it was, I nearly fainted. That would be me. I would have to be lowered down like that, and I would never put a kagoul on again. Oh the shame, the terror, the panic.

What I should have been worrying about was the time. As the last of the unfortunate potato woman's party hopped down from the top, God decided we should suffer a little more, and a massive front of cloud swept in and once again obscured the top. This time we waited. We had little choice. There was no way at all we could come back again the next day, since our schedule was already miles out. If we didn't climb it that afternoon, we would have to drop it from the programme. We waited until 5.30, when

Ross looked at his watch and said it was nearly time to get moving, but we had seen little breaks in the cloud so we stayed put. At 5.45 a substantial break in the clouds appeared and revealed the top to us again. The rock was dry, the hole in the clouds looked like it might last for half an hour, so we leapt to it. Once again, Ross was not a happy man.

Ross went up first, with nothing to stop him falling off and mashing himself on the hard rock except balance, nerve and leg muscles like tights stuffed with grapefruits.

In all the things I have been required to do in the line of television duty I have never been more genuinely terrified. Brian fitted Ross and I with personal radio mikes since his boom, the furry microphone on a stick you see sound men waving at politicians outside court rooms, would never pick up our words from such a distance. The result was not a lively conversation between Ross and I as we merrily claimed the summit, but a tape full of me making noises like a cat in a liquidiser, while Ross bellowed at me from above. Later in the editing suite, I had to remove most of the sound from the pictures because of my hideously sharp breathing, whimpering and swearing. It doesn't take much to make you forget you're supposed to be presenting a television programme, and as soon as I started to climb I was oblivious to everything except the 3,000-foot drop and the fact that I couldn't find anything to hold on to.

But we did it, and as I abseiled down there wasn't a happier woman in Scotland. It was now nearly 6.30 p.m. and the cloud was starting to thicken again. We knew it was late, but Ali and Angus wanted to climb to the top. Since they had come this far twice in two days it seemed unfair to say no, so Ross went back up and let the pair of them take their turn. Yes, thank you, readers, I know how stupid this seems to you as you sit tutting at this folly from the safety of a comfy chair, but it didn't feel so outrageous at the time. It was 7 p.m. when we started to descend, and we knew if we made it down off the ridge on to the lower grassy slopes by 7.45, we would be fine. Sadly the mist decided to audition for a part in a horror movie, and before we reached the crucial turning on the ridge that led down on to the plateau, visibility was down to about 20 feet.

We made an error. For some reason we turned and headed south, missing the gap in the rocks that we needed to find, and headed downhill, totally unaware we were heading for the cliffs above Coire Lagan. As it grew darker, the way became more impassable, until we were hanging on to a cliff by our fingertips in near blackness. The compass wouldn't work

The Inaccessible and almost invisible Pinnacle
OPPOSITE: A scrambler out of her depth

184

on these magnetic rocks, and we had no idea what lay below us. When somebody dislodged a rock with their feet and it fell for an uncomfortably long time in silence before smashing apart hundreds of feet below, we knew we were in trouble. Ross made our choice clear. We would have to climb all the way back up on to the ridge if we were to have any chance of finding the path. It was either that or we stayed put and spent the night on the mountain. Nobody was keen on the second option, so we retraced our steps as best we could and regained the ridge. By a huge stroke of luck, we found the path as the very last milky drops of light faded from the mist. Once again it was a descent in complete darkness, aided by three head torches among seven. I had left mine in my car.

The scramble down the rocks to the safety of the grass was something nobody will forget, or indeed let me forget when I ask them to work with me again. People fell every few minutes, tripping and stumbling through exhaustion and blindness, and on reaching the grassy slopes below the crags, trips had turned into full-scale, head-first tumbles into the heather. Nobody got back to the car without having partaken in amateur acrobatics that resulted in a face full of peat.

As we sat over some soup at the Sligachan Hotel at quarter to eleven at night, the crew glaring at me with naked accusation in their eyes, I fought back the tears and a genuine regret that I had not gone to Scottish Television with an idea for a chat show in a warm studio. Cheating has a lot to offer.

HELICOPTER PHOBIA

After every climb, we needed to return to the mountain on a completely separate day, drop me at the places I had delivered my pieces to camera, film it and try and cut it all together as if it happened at the same time. The difficulties in that plan are enormous, not least that Scotland rarely offers two days of weather alike. The difficulty for me was that I had to jump in and out of a helicopter that was not always able to make a completely stable landing on two runners, on top of terrifying ridges and peaks.

Dominic, our pilot from PLM Helicopters, gave me a brief safety run-down pointing out with some glee all the things that could go wrong, and reminding me that it was at my own risk. As an afterthought he added, 'Oh, and try to remember not to run downhill at me to get back in. You'll probably decapitate yourself.'

I was hardly likely to forget. In fact I tossed and turned at night thinking of the bill PLM would land us with for clogging up their blades with bits of my face.

But who could complain about flying all over Scotland's mountains, leaping in and out at all the most exciting places on a hill? There was one factor, however, that drove me wild with rage. Every time we returned to a hill with the helicopter and dropped me at the summit, there were always two or three walkers sitting at the cairn, watching the proceedings sardonically. As soon as I hopped out, I always went to apologise to them for spoiling their peace. It's not so great walking for four hours to escape humanity, only to find a dirty great helicopter hovering ten feet above your flask before depositing someone who runs around like a maniac shouting into a walkie talkie. So I would nip over, tell them what we were up to and grovel a bit. Their response never varied. 'So that's how you do these shows, is it? Most of us have to walk up.'

Given the experiences of the shoot thus far, my first instinct was to resort to swift and immediate violence, but these were viewers and one is contractually bound to be reasonably pleasant. So I carried on throughout the summer like an apprentice Anneka Rice, taking good-natured abuse from every Munro-climber in Britain, with my teeth gritted. I did at one point contemplate having a card printed that I could simply hand to the doubting Thomases on the slopes. It would read, 'Shut your face, dog breath. I've climbed it twice already.' On reflection, however, I decided it might not show advanced public relations skills on my part and settled on smiling and waving instead.

Helicopters are expensive things, and since our budget was as tight as Billy Idol's pants, it was important to get the most out of our time. This meant that after the shot had been completed of me walking at a leisurely pace along a mountain top, trying to remember what I did three weeks ago when we filmed it from the ground, I would have to sprint back to the chopper to get to the next location without delay. Wasting time getting in and out meant money lost. By the time we were at location two, my heart was trying to knock a hole in my vest and I was starting to hallucinate. The worst one of all, of course, was a return to the In Pin. This meant being dumped at the base and climbing the whole thing again, but this time with a helicopter roaring only yards away. The only delight was on my return to the car park. The chopper dumped me, still wearing all the climbing gear, and went back to pick up Ross. I spoke to the pilot with a walkie talkie and

OVERLEAF:
Buzzing the Inaccessible
Pinnacle

187

reminded them to get a shot of the path on the way back down. As I started to undo all the strange and mysterious straps, a man approached me in a very polite, reverential way. I'm not used to being approached like this. Normally people either shout 'Hoi, are you that thin bint on the telly?' or they simply point and laugh. This man clearly had some respect.

'Excuse me,' he said, practically bowing. Things were looking up in ego land. 'Is there an exercise on today, or is it a real emergency?'

I looked blankly at him, trying to decipher the sentence. With enormous disappointment, my brain collated the information and came back with the solution that this man thought I was a Mountain Rescue person. I caught sight of myself reflected in the car window, peroxide blonde hair, pink lipstick and legs like sticks, and couldn't help wondering what this man must imagine the rest of the Mountain Rescue team might look like.

'No. No emergency,' was all I could manage, but he had certainly made my day. I strutted around in the car park in a manly fashion for a few more minutes before taking off the climbing gear, just in case somebody else thought I was in the Mountain Rescue team. I was on the point of thinking of growing a beard when somebody pointed and laughed. It was business as usual and I hid in the car.